THE SYMPATHY OF RELIGIONS.

AN ADDRESS,

DELIVERED AT HORTICULTURAL HALL, BOSTON,

FEBRUARY 6, 1870.

BY

THOMAS WENTWORTH HIGGINSON.

BOSTON:

REPRINTED FROM THE RADICAL.

OFFICE, 25 BROMFIELD STREET.

1871.

THE

SYMPATHY OF RELIGIONS.

BY THOMAS WENTWORTH HIGGINSON.

OUR true religious life begins when we discover that there is an Inner Light, not infallible but invaluable, which "lighteth every man that cometh into the world." Then we have something to steer by; and it is chiefly this, and not an anchor, that we need. The human soul, like any other noble vessel, was not built to be anchored, but to sail. An anchorage may, indeed, be at times a temporary need, in order to make some special repairs, or to take fresh cargo in; yet the natural destiny of both ship and soul is not the harbor, but the ocean; to cut with even keel the vast and beautiful expanse; to pass from island on to island of more than Indian balm, or to continents fairer than Columbus won; or, best of all, steering close to the wind, to extract motive power from the greatest obstacles. Men must forget the eternity through which they have yet to sail, when they talk of anchoring here upon this bank and shoal of time. It would be a tragedy to see the shipping of the world whitening the seas no more, and idly riding at anchor in Atlantic ports; but it would be more tragic to see a world of souls fascinated into a fatal repose and renouncing their destiny of motion.

And as with individuals, so with communities. The great historic religions of the world are not so many stranded hulks left to perish. The best of them are all in motion. All over the world the divine influence moves men. There is a sympathy in religions, and this sympathy is shown alike in their origin, their records, and their progress. Men are ceasing to disbelieve, and learning to believe more. I have worshiped in an Evangelical church when thousands rose to their feet at the motion of one hand. I have worshiped in a Roman Catholic church when the lifting of one finger broke the motionless multitude into twinkling motion, till the magic sign was made, and all was still once more. But I never for an instant have supposed that this concentrated moment of devotion was more holy or more beautiful than when one cry from a minaret hushes a Mohammedan city to prayer, or when, at sunset, the low invocation, "Oh! the gem in the lotus — oh! the gem in the lotus," goes murmuring, like the cooing of many doves, across the vast surface of Thibet. True, "the gem in the lotus" means nothing to us, but it means as much to the angels as "the Lamb of God," for it is a symbol of aspiration.

Every year brings new knowledge of the religions of the world, and every step in knowledge brings out the sympathy between them. They all show the same aim, the same symbols, the same forms, the same weaknesses, the same aspirations. Looking at these points of unity, we might say there is but one religion under many forms, whose essential creed is the Fatherhood of God, and the Brotherhood of Man,— disguised by corruptions, symbolized by mythologies, ennobled by virtues, degraded by vices, but still the same. Or if, passing to a closer analysis, we observe the shades of difference, we shall find in these varying faiths the several instruments which perform what Cudworth calls "the Symphony of Religions." And though some may stir like drums, and others soothe like flutes, and others like violins command the whole range of softness and of strength, yet they are all alike instruments, and nothing in any one of them is so wondrous as the great laws of sound which equally control them all.

"Amid so much war and contest and variety of opinion," said Maximus Tyrius, "you will find one consenting conviction in every land, that there is one God, the King and Father of all."

"God being one," said Aristotle, "only receives various names from the various manifestations we perceive." "Sovereign God," said Cleanthes, in that sublime prayer which Paul quoted, "whom men invoke under many names, and who rulest alone, . . . it is to thee that all nations should address themselves, for we all are thy children." So Origen, the Christian Father, frankly says that no man can be blamed for calling God's name in Egyptian, nor in Scythian, nor in such other language as he best knows.*

To say that different races worship different Gods, is like saying that they are warmed by different suns. The names differ, but the sun is the same, and so is God. As there is but one source of light and warmth, so there is but one source of religion. To this all nations testify alike. We have yet but a part of our Holy Bible. The time will come when, as in the middle ages, all pious books will be called sacred scriptures, *Scripturæ Sacræ*. From the most remote portions of the earth, from the Vedas and the Sagas, from Plato and Zoroaster, Confucius and Mohammed, from the Emperor Marcus Antoninus and the slave Epictetus, from the learned Alexandrians and the ignorant Galla negroes, there will be gathered hymns and prayers and maxims in which every religious soul may unite, — the magnificent liturgy of the human race.

The greatest of modern scholars, Von Humboldt, asserted in middle life and repeated the assertion in old age, that "all positive religions contain three distinct parts. First, a code of morals, very fine, and nearly the same in all. Second, a geological dream, and, third, a myth or historical novelette, which last becomes the most important of all." And though this observation may be somewhat roughly stated, its essential truth is seen when we compare the different religions of the world, side by side. With such startling points of similarity, where is the difference? The main difference lies here, that each fills some blank space in its creed with the name of a different teacher. For in-

* This is Cudworth's interpretation, but he has rather strained the passage, which must be that beginning, *Οὐδὲν οὖν οἶμαι διαφέρειν* (Adv. Celsum, v.). The passages from Aristotle and Cleanthes are in Stobæus. Compare Maximus Tyrius, Diss. I.: *Θεὸς εἷς πάντων βασιλεὺς καὶ πατὴρ.*

stance, the Oriental Parsee wears a fine white garment, bound around him with a certain knot; and whenever this knot is undone, at morning or night, he repeats the four main points of his creed, which are as follows: —

"To believe in one God, and hope for mercy from him only."

"To believe in a future state of existence."

"To do as you would be done by."

Thus far the Parsee keeps on the universal ground of religion. Then he drops into the language of his sect and adds, —

"To believe in Zoroaster as lawgiver, and to hold his writings sacred."

The creed thus furnishes a formula for all religions. It might be printed in blank like a circular, leaving only the closing name to be filled in.* For Zoroaster read Christ, and you have Christianity; read Buddha, and you have Budhhism; read Mohammed, and you have Mohammedanism. Each of these, in short, is Natural Religion *plus* an individual name. It is by insisting on that *plus* that each religion stops short of being universal.

In this religion of the human race, thus variously disguised, we find everywhere the same leading features. The same great doctrines, good or bad, — regeneration, predestination, atonement, the future life, the final judgment, the Divine Reason or Logos, and the Trinity. The same religious institutions, — monks, missionaries, priests, and pilgrims. The same ritual, — prayers, liturgies, sacrifices, sermons, hymns. The same implements, — frankincense, candles, holy water, relics, amulets, votive offerings. The same symbols, — the cross, the ball, the triangle, the serpent, the all-seeing eye, the halo of rays, the tree of life. The same saints, angels, and martyrs. The same holiness attached to particular cities, rivers, and mountains. The same prophecies and miracles, — the dead restored and evil spirits cast out. The self-same holy days; for Easter and Christmas were kept as spring and autumn festivals, centuries before our era, by Egyptians, Persians, Saxons, Romans. The same artistic designs, since the mother and child stand depicted,

* Compare Augustine, De Vera Relig., c. iv.: "Paucis mutatis verbis atque sententiis Christiani fierent." The Parsee creed is given as above in a valuble article in Martin's Colonial Magazine, No. 18.

not only in the temples of Europe, but in those of Etruria and Arabia, Egypt and Thibet. In ancient Christian art, the evangelists were represented with the same heads of eagles, oxen, and lions, upon which we gaze with amazement in Egyptian tombs. Nay, the very sects and subdivisions of all historic religions have been the same, and each supplies us with mystic and rationalist, formalist and philanthropist, ascetic and epicurean. The simple fact is, that all these things are as indigenous as grass and mosses; they spring up in every soil, and only the microscope can tell them apart.

And, as all these inevitably recur, so comes back again and again the idea of incarnation, — the Divine Man. Here, too, all religions sympathize, and, with slight modifications, each is the copy of the other. As in the dim robing-rooms of foreign churches are kept rich stores of sacred vestments, ready to be thrown over every successive generation of priests, so the world has kept in memory the same stately traditions to decorate each new Messiah. He is predicted by prophecy, hailed by sages, born of a virgin, attended by miracle, borne to heaven without tasting death, and with promise of return. Zoroaster and Confucius have no human father. Osiris is the Son of God, he is called the Revealer of Life and Light; he first teaches one chosen race; he then goes with his apostles to teach the Gentiles, conquering the world by peace; he is slain by evil powers; after death he descends into hell, then rises again, and presides at the last judgment of all mankind: those who call upon his name shall be saved. Buddha is born of a virgin; his name means the Word, the Logos, but he is known more tenderly as the Saviour of Man; he embarrasses his teachers, when a child, by his understanding and his answers; he is tempted in the wilderness, when older; he goes with his apostles to redeem the world; he abolishes caste and cruelty, and teaches forgiveness; he receives among his followers outcasts whom Pharisaic pride despises, and he only says, "My law is a law of mercy to all." Slain by enemies, he descends into hell, rising without tasting death, and still lives to make intercession for man.

These are the recognized properties of religious tradition; the beautiful garments belong not to the individual, but the race. It is the drawback on all human greatness that it makes itself deified. Even of Jesus it was said sincerely by the Platonic philosopher Porphyry, "That noble soul, who has ascended into heaven, has by a certain fatality become an occasion of error." The inequality of gifts is a problem not yet solved, and there is always a craving for some miracle to explain it. Men set up their sublime representatives as so many spiritual athletes, and measure them. "See, this one is six inches taller; those six inches prove him divine." But because men surpass us, or surpass everybody, shall we hold them separate from the race? Construct the race as you will, somebody must stand at the head, in virtue as in intellect. Shall we deify Shakespeare? Because we may begin upon his treasury of wisdom almost before we enjoy any other book, and can hold to it longer, and read it all our lives, from those earnest moments when we demand the very core of thought, down to moments of sickness and sadness when nothing else captivates; because we may go the rounds of all literature, and grow surfeited with every other great author, and learn a dozen languages and a score of philosophical systems, and travel the wide world over, and come back to Shakespeare at length, fresh as ever, and begin at the beginning of his infinite meanings once more,— are we therefore to consider him as separated from mortality? Are we to raise him to the heavens, as in the magnificent eulogium of Keats, who heads creation with "things real, as sun, stars, and passages of Shakespeare"? Or are we to erect into a creed the bold words I once heard an enthusiast soberly say, "that it is impossible to think of Shakespeare as a man"? Or shall we reverently own, that, as man's humility first bids him separate himself from these his great superiors, so his faith and hope bring him back to them and renew the tie. It paralyzes my intellect if I doubt whether Shakespeare was a man; it paralyzes my whole spiritual nature if I doubt whether Jesus was.

Therefore I believe that all religion is natural, all revealed. What faith in humanity springs up, what trust in God, when one recognizes the sympathy of religions! Every race believes in a Creator and Governor of the world, in whom devout souls recognize a Father also. Every race believes in immortality. Every race recognizes in its religious precepts the brotherhood of man. The whole gigantic system of caste in Hindostan has grown up in defiance of the Vedas, which are now being invoked to abolish them. The Heetopades of Vishnu Sarman forbid caste. "Is this one of our tribe or a stranger? is the calculation of the narrow-minded; but, to those of a noble disposition, the earth itself is but one family." "What is religion?" says elsewhere the same book, and answers, "Tenderness toward all creatures." "He is my beloved of whom mankind are not afraid and who of mankind is not afraid," says the Bhagvat Geeta. "Kesava is pleased with him who does good to others, . . . who is always desirous of the welfare of all creatures," says the Vishnu Purana. In Confucius it is written, "My doctrine is simple and easy to understand;" and his chief disciple adds, "It consists only in having the heart right and in loving one's neighbor as one's self." When he was asked, "Is there one word which may serve as a rule of practice for all one's life?" he answered, "Is not 'Reciprocity' such a word? What you wish done to yourself, do to others." By some translators the rule is given in a negative form, in which it is also found in the Jewish Talmud (Rabbi Hillel), "Do not to another what thou wouldst not he should do to thee; this is the sum of the law." So Thales, when asked for a rule of life, taught, "That which thou blamest in another, do not thyself." "Thou shalt love thy neighbor as thyself," said the Hebrew book of Leviticus. Iamblichus tells us that Pythagoras taught "the love of all to all." "To live is not to live for one's self alone, let us help one another," said the Greek dramatist Menander; and the Roman dramatist Terence, following him, brought down the applause of the whole theatre by the saying, "I am a man; I count nothing human foreign to me." "Give bread to a stranger," said Quintilian, "in the name of the universal brotherhood which binds together all men under the common father of nature." "What good man will look on any suffering as foreign to himself?" said the Latin satirist Juvenal. "This sympathy is what distinguishes us from brutes," he adds. The poet Lucan predicted a time when warlike weapons should be laid aside, and all men love one another. "Nature has inclined us to love men," said Cicero, "and this is the foundation of the law." He also described his favorite virtue of justice as "devoting itself wholly to the good of others." Seneca said, "We are members of one great body. Nature planted in us a mutual love, and fitted us for a social life. We must consider that we were born for the good of the whole." "Love mankind," wrote Marcus Antoninus, summing it all up in two words; while the loving soul of Epictetus extended the sphere of mutual affection beyond this earth, holding that "the universe is but one great city, full of beloved ones, divine and human, by nature endeared to each other." *

This sympathy of religions extends even to the loftiest virtues, — the forgiveness of injuries, the love of enemies and the overcoming of evil with good. "The wise man," said the Chinese Lao-tse, "avenges his injuries with benefits." "Hatred," says a Buddhist sacred book, the Dhammapada, "does not cease by hatred at any time; hatred ceases by love; this is the eternal rule." "To overcome evil with good is good, and to resist evil by evil is evil," says a Mohammedan manual of ethics.

* See Vishnu Sarman (tr. by Johnson), pp. 16, 28. Bhagvat Geeta (tr. by Wilkins), ch. 12. Vishnu Purana (tr. by Wilson), p. 291. Confucius, Lun-yu (tr. by Pauthier), ch. iv. § 16. Also Davis' Chinese, ii. 50. [Legge's Confucian Analects, xv. 23, gives the negative form.] Thales, in Diogenes Laertius, B. I., § 36: Πῶς ἂν ἄριστα καὶ δικαιότατα βιώσαιμεν; ἐὰν ἃ τοῖς ἄλλοις ἐπιτιμῶμεν, αὐτοὶ μὴ δρῶμεν. Stobæus reads instead (c. 43), ὅσα νεμεσεῖς τον πλησίον, αὐτὸς μὴ ποίει. Leviticus xix. 18. Iamblichus de Pythag. vita, c. 16 and 33: Φιλίαν δὲ διαφανέστατα πάντων πρὸς ἅπαντας Πυθαγόρας παρέδωκε. Terence, Heaut. I., 1, 25: "Homo sum, humani nihil a me alienum puto." Quintilian, Declamations, quoted by Denis. Juvenal, Sat. xv. 140–142: —

> "Quis enim bonus . . .
> Ulla aliena sibi credat mala?"

Lucan, Pharsalia, I. 60, 61: —

> "Tunc genus humanum positis sibi consulat armis
> Inque vicem gens omnis amet."

Cicero, de Legibus i. 15: "Nam haec nascuntur ex eo, quia natura propensi sumus ad diligendos homines, quod fundamentum juris est." Also de Republica, iii. 7, 7 (fragment): "Quae virtus, praeter ceteras, tota se ad alienas porrigit utilitates et explicat." Marcus Antoninus, vii. 31: Φίλησον τὸν ἀνθρώπινον γένος. Epictetus, B. III., c. xxiv.: Ὅτι ὁ κόσμος οὗτος μία πόλις ἐστὶ . . . πάντα δὲ φίλων μεστὰ, πρῶτον μὲν Θεῶν, εἶτα καὶ ἀνθρώπων, φύσει πρὸς ἀλλήλοις ᾠκειωμένων.

"Turn not away from a sinner, but look on him with compassion," says Saadi's Gulistan. "If thine enemy hunger, give him bread to eat; if he thirst, give him water to drink," said the Hebrew proverb. "He who commits injustice is ever made more wretched than he who suffers it," said Plato, and adds, "It is never right to return an injury." "No one will dare maintain," said Aristotle, "that it is better to do injustice than to bear it." "We should do good to our enemy," said Cleobulus, "and make him our friend." "Speak not evil to a friend, nor even to an enemy," said Pittacus, one of the Seven Wise Men. "It is more beautiful," said Valerius Maximus, "to overcome injury by the power of kindness than to oppose to it the obstinacy of hatred." Maximus Tyrius has a special chapter on the treatment of injuries, and concludes: "If he who injures does wrong, he who returns the injury does equally wrong." Plutarch, in his essay, "How to profit by our enemies," bids us sympathize with them in affliction and aid their needs. "A philosopher, when smitten, must love those who smite him, as if he were the father, the brother, of all men," said Epictetus. "It is peculiar to man," said Marcus Antoninus, "to love even those who do wrong. . . . Ask thyself daily to how many ill-minded persons thou hast shown a kind disposition." He compares the wise and humane soul to a spring of pure water which blesses even him who curses it; and the Oriental story likens such a soul to the sandal-wood tree, which imparts its fragrance even to the axe that cuts it down.*

* Dhammapada (tr. by Max Müller), in Rogers' Buddhagosha's Parables. Akhlak-i-Jalaly (tr. by Thompson), p. 441. Saadi's Gulistan (tr. by Ross), p. 240; (tr. by Gladwin, Am. ed.), p. 209. Proverbs xxv. 21. Plato, Gorgias, § 78: *'Αέι τὸν ἀδικοὐντα τον ἀδικουμένου αθλιώτερον ειναι.* Crito, § 10: *'Ως οὐδέποτε ὀρθῶς ἔχοντος οὔτε του ἀδικεῖν οὔτε του ἀνταδυκεῖν.* Cleobulus in Diog. Laertius, B. I., § 91: *"Σλεγέ τε τὸν φίλον δεῖν εὐεργετεῖν, ὅπως ᾐ μᾶλλον φίλος. τὸν δὲ ἐχθρὸν, φίλον ποιεῖν.* Pittacus in Diog. Laertius, B. I., § 78: *Φίλον μὴ λέγειν κακῶς, ἀλλὰ μηδὲ εχθρόν.* Val. Maximus, iv. 2, 4: "Quia speciosius aliquanto injuriae beneficiis vincuntur quam mutui odii pertinacia pensantur." Max. Tyrius, Diss. II.: *Κάι μὲν εἰ ὁ ἀδικῶν κακῶς ποιεῖ, ὁ ἀντιποιῶν κακῶς οὐδὲν ἧττον ποιεῖ κακῶς, κἄν ἀμύνηται.* Plutarch's Morals (tr. by Goodwin, I., 293. Epictetus, B. IV., c. 23: *Δαίρεσθαι δεῖ αὐτὸν, ὡς ὄνον, καὶ δαιρόμενον φιλεῖν αὐτοὺς τοὺς δαίροντας, ὡς πατέρα πάντων, ὡς ἀδελφόν.* Marcus Antoninus, Medit. v. 31. vii. 22: **"Ιδιον ἀνθρωπον φίλον και τοὺς πταίοντας. . . . Εἰς ὅσους δὲ ἀγνώμονας ἐυγνώμων εγενές.**

How it cheers and enlarges us to hear of these great thoughts and know that the Divine has never been without a witness on earth! How it must sadden the soul to disbelieve them. Worse yet to be in a position where one has to hope that they may not be correctly reported,— that one by one they may be explained away. A prosecuting attorney once told me that the most painful part of his position was that he had to hope that every man he prosecuted would be proved a villain. What is the painful circumstance in Mrs. Stowe's Byron controversy? That she is obliged to hope that the character of a sister woman, hitherto stainless, may be hopelessly blackened. But what is this to their position who are bound to hope that the character of humanity will be blackened by wholesale, who are compelled to resist every atom of light that history reveals. For instance, as the great character of Buddha has come out from the darkness, within fifty years, how these reluctant people have struggled against it, still desiring to escape. "Save us, O God!" they have seemed to say, "from the distress of believing that so many years ago there was a sublime human life." Show such persons that the great religious ideas and maxims are as old as literature; and how they resist the knowledge! "Surely it is not so bad as that," they say. "Is there not a possibility of a mistranslation? Let us see the text, explore the lexicon; is there no labor, no toil, by which we can convince ourselves that there is a mistake? Anything rather than believe that there is a light which lighteth every man that cometh into the world."

For this purpose the very facts of history must be suppressed or explained away. Sir George Mackenzie, in his "Travels in Iceland," says that the clergy prevented till 1630, with "mistaken zeal," the publication of the Scandinavian Eddas. Huc, the Roman Catholic Missionary, described in such truthful colors the religious influence of Buddhism in Thibet that his book was put in the *index expurgatorius* at Rome. Balmes, a learned Roman Catholic writer, declares that "Christianity is stripped of a portion of its honors" if we trace back any high standard of female purity to the ancient Germans; and so he coolly sets aside as "poetical" the plain statements of the accurate

Tacitus. If we are to believe the accounts given of the Jewish Essenes by Josephus, De Quincey thinks, the claims made by Christianity are annihilated. "If Essenism could make good its pretensions, there, at one blow, would be an end of Christianity, which, in that case, is not only superseded as an idle repetition of a religious system already published, but as a criminal plagiarism. Nor can the wit of man evade the conclusion." He accordingly attempts to explain away the testimony of Josephus.*

And what makes this exclusiveness the more repulsive is its modernness. Paul himself quoted from the sublime hymn of Cleanthes to prove to the Greeks that they too recognized the Fatherhood of God. The early Christian apologists, living face to face with the elder religions, made no exclusive claims. Tertullian declared the soul to be an older authority than prophecy, and its voice the gift of God from the beginning. Justin Martyr said, "Those who live according to Reason are Christians, though you may call them atheists. . . . Such among the Greeks were Socrates and Heraclitus and the rest. They who have made or do make Reason (Logos) their rule of life are Christians and men without fear and trembling." "The same God," said Clement, "to whom we owe the Old and New Testaments gave also to the Greeks their Greek philosophy by which the Almighty is glorified among the Greeks." Lactantius declared that the ancient philosophers "attained the full truth and the whole mystery of religion." "One would suppose," said Minucius Felix, "either that the Christians were philosophers, or the philosophers Christians." "What is now called the Christian religion," said Augustine, "has existed among the ancients, and was not absent from the beginning of the human race, until Christ came in the flesh; from which time the true religion, which existed already, began to be called Christian." Jerome said that "the knowledge of God was present by nature

* Balmes, Protestantism and Catholicity, c. xxvii. and note. Mackenzie's Iceland, p. 26. De Quincey, Autobiographical Sketches, p. 17, and Essay on the Essenes. The condemnation of Huc's book is mentioned by Max Müller, Chips, &c., I., 187.

in all, nor was there any one born without God, or who had not in himself the seeds of all virtues." *

How few modern sects reach even this point of impartiality! The usual course of theologians is to deny, and to deny with fury, that any such sympathy of religions exists. "There never was a time," says a distinguished European preacher, "when there did not exist an infinite gulf between the ideas of the ancients and the ideas of Christianity. There is an end of Christianity if men agree in thinking the contrary." And an eminent Unitarian preacher in America, Rev. A. P. Peabody, says, "If the truths of Christianity are intuitive and self-evident, how is it that they formed no part of any man's consciousness till the advent of Christ?" How can any one look history in the face, how can any man open even the dictionary of any ancient language, and yet say this? What word sums up the highest Christian virtue if not *philanthropy?* And yet the word is a Greek word, and was used in the same sense before Christendom existed.†

* "Nec hoc ullis Mosis libris debent. Ante anima quam prophetia. Animæ enim a primordio conscientia Dei dos est."—*Tertullian, adv. Marcion,* I, 10.

Οἱ μετὰ Λόγου βιώσαντες χριστιανοί εἰσι, κἂν ἄθεοι ἐνομίσθησαν, οἷον ἐν Ἕλλησι μὲν Σωκράτης καὶ Ἡράκλειτος καὶ οἱ ὅμοιοι αὐτοῖς, κ. τ. λ.—*Justin Martyr, Apol.* i. 46.

Πρὸς δὲ καὶ ὅτι ὁ αὐτὸς θεὸς ἀμφοῖν ταῖν διαθήκαιν χορηγὸς, ὁ καὶ τῆς Ἑλληνικῆς φιλοσοφίας δοτὴρ τοῖς Ἕλλησιν, δι ἧς ὁ παντοκράτωρ παρ' Ἕλλησι δοξάζεται, παρέστησεν, δῆλον δὲ κἀνθένδε.—*Clem. Alex. Strom.*, VI. v. 42.

"Totam igitur veritatem et omne divinæ religionis arcanum philosophi attigerunt."—*Lactantius, Inst.* viii. 7.

"Ut quivis arbitretur, aut nunc Christianos philosophos esse, aut philosophos fuisse jam tunc Christianos."—*Minucius Felix, Octavius,* c. xx.

"Res ipsa, quæ nunc religio Christiana nuncupatur, erat apud antiquos, nec defuit ab initio generis humani, quousque Christus veniret in carnem, unde vera religio, quæ jam erat, cœpit appellari Christiana."—*Augustine, Retr.*, i. 13.

"Natura omnibus Dei inesse notitiam, nec quemquam sine Deo nasci, et non habere in se semina sapientiæ et justitiæ reliquarumque virtutum." —*Hieron., Comm. in Gal.*, I., 1, 15.

† Ἐγὼ δὲ φοβοῦμαι μὴ ὑπὸ φιλανθρωπίας δοκῶ αὐτοῖς ὅ το περ ἔχω εκκεχυμένως παντὶ ἀνδρὶ λεγειν.—*Plato, Euthyphron,* § 3.

"Quodque a Græcis φιλανθρωπία dicitur, et significat dexteritatem quandam benevolentiamque erga omnes homines promiscuam."—*Aulus Gellius,* B. XIII., c. xvi. 1.

How much more frank and scholarlike are the admissions of Dean Mil-

Fortunately there have always been men whose larger minds could adapt themselves to the truth instead of narrowing the truth to them. In William Penn's "No Cross No Crown," one-half the pages are devoted to the religious testimony of Christians, and one-half to that of the non-Christian world. The writings of the most learned of English Catholics, Digby, are a treasure-house of ancient religion, and the conflict between the bigot and the scholar makes him deliciously inconsistent. He states a doctrine, illustrates it from the schoolmen or the fathers, proudly claims it as being monopolized by the Christian church, and ends by citing a parallel passage from Plato or Æschylus! "The ancient poets," he declares, "seem never to have conceived the idea of a spirit of resignation which would sanctify calamity;" and accordingly he quotes Aristotle's assertion, that "suffering becomes beautiful when any one bears great calamities with cheerfulness, not through insensibility, but through greatness of mind." "There is not a passage in the classics," he declares, "which recognizes the beauty of holiness and Christian mildness;" and in the next breath he remarks, that Homer's description of Patroclus furnishes language which might convey an idea of that mildness of manner which belonged to men in Christian ages." And he closes his eloquent picture of the faith of the middle ages in immortality by attributing to the monks and friars the dying language of Socrates, that "a man who has spent his life in the study of philosophy ought to take courage in his death, and to be full of hope that he is about to possess the greatest good that can be obtained, which will be in his possession as soon as he dies;" and much more of that serene and sublime wisdom. Yet all this is done in a manner so absolutely free from sophistry, the conflict between the scholar and the churchman is so innocent and transparent, that one forgives it in Digby. In most writers on these subjects there is greater bigotry, without the learning which in his case

man: "If we were to glean from the later Jewish writings, from the beautiful aphorisms of other Oriental nations, which we cannot fairly trace to Christian sources, and from the Platonic and Stoic philosophy their more striking precepts, we might find, perhaps, a counterpart to almost all the moral sayings of Jesus."—*Hist. Christianity*, B. I., c. iv., § 3.

makes it endurable, because it supplies the means for its own correction.*

And, if it is thus hard to do historical justice, it is far harder to look with candor upon contemporary religions. Thus the Jesuit Father Ripa thought that Satan had created the Buddhist religion on purpose to bewilder the Christian church. There we see a creed possessing more votaries than any in the world, numbering nearly one-third of the human race. Its traditions go back to a founder whose record is stainless and sublime. It has the doctrine of the Real Presence, the Madonna and Child, the invocation of the dead, monasteries and pilgrimages, celibacy and tonsure, relics, rosaries, and holy water. Wherever it has spread, it has broken down the barrier of caste. It teaches that all men are brethren, and makes them prove it by their acts; it diffuses gentleness and self-sacrificing benevolence. "It has become," as Neander admits, "to many tribes of people a means of transition from the wildest barbarism to semi-civilization." Tennent, living amid the lowest form of it in Ceylon, says that its code of morals is "second only to that of Christianity itself," and enjoins "every conceivable virtue and excellence." It is coming among us, represented by many of the Chinese, and a San-Francisco merchant, a Christian of the Episcopal Church, told me that, on conversing with their educated men, he found in them a religious faith quite as enlightened as his own. Shall we not rejoice in this consoling discovery? "Yes," said the simple-hearted Abbé Huc: so he published his account of Buddhism, and saw it excommunicated. "No!" said Father Ripa, "it is the invention of the devil!" †

With a steady wave of progress Mohammedanism is sweeping through Africa, where Christianity scarcely advances a step. Wherever Mohammedanism reaches, schools and libraries are

* Digby's Ages of Faith, II., 174, 178, 287–289, &c. Digby's inconsistent method has ample precedent in the early Christian apologists. Tertullian, for instance, glorifies the Christian martyrs, and then, to show that they are not foolish or desperate men, cites the precedents of Regulus, Zeno, Mutius Scævola, and many others (Apol. c. 50)!

† Compare Neander (Am. tr.), I., 450. Huc's Thibet, II., 50. Tennent's Christianity in Ceylon, pp. 219, 220.

established, gambling and drunkenness cease, theft and falsehood diminish, polygamy is limited, woman begins to be elevated and has property rights guaranteed; and, instead of witnessing human sacrifices, you see the cottager reading the Koran at her door, like the Christian cottager in Cowper's description. "Its gradual extension," says an eye-witness, "is gradually but surely modifying the negro. . . . Within the last half century the humanizing influence of the Koran is acknowledged by all who are acquainted with the interior tribes." * So in India, Mohammed-

* Capt. Canot, pp. 153, 180, 181. Wilson's Western Africa, 75, 79, 92. Richardson's Great Desert, II., 63, 129. Johnstone's Abyssinia, I., 267; Allen's Niger Expedition, I., 383. Du Chaillu, Ashango Land, xiii., 129. Barth, *passim*, especially (I., 310): "That continual struggle, which always continuing further and further, seems destined to overpower the nations at the very equator, if Christianity does not presently step in to dispute the ground with it." He says "that a great part of the Berbers of the desert were once Christians, and that they afterwards changed their religion and adopted Islam" (I., 197, 198). He represents the slave merchants of the interior as complaining that the Mohammedans of Tunis have abolished slavery, but that Christians still continue it (I., 465). "It is difficult to decide how a Christian government is to deal with these countries, where none but Mohammedans maintain any sort of government" (II., 196). "There is a vital principle in Islam, which has only to be brought out by a reformer to accomplish great things" (I., 164).

Reade, in his Savage Africa, discusses the subject fully in a closing chapter, and concludes thus: "Mohammed, a servant of God, redeemed the eastern world. His followers are now redeeming Africa. . . . Let us aid the Mohammedans in their great work, the redemption of Africa. . . . In every Mohammedan town there is a public school and a public library." He complains that Christianity utterly fails to check theft, but Mohamedanism stops it entirely (pp. 135, 579, English ed.).

For Asiatic Mohammedanism see Sleeman's Recollections, II., 164, and compare Tennent's Christianity in Ceylon, p. 330, and Max Müller's Chips from a German Workshop, II., 351. The London Spectator, in April, 1869, stated that "Mohammedanism gains thousands of converts every year," and thus described the activity of its organization, the statement being condensed in the Boston Journal: "Of all these societies, the largest, the most powerful, the most widely diffused, is the Mohammedan population. Everywhere it has towns, villages, temples, places within which no infidel foot ever is or can be set. Its missionaries wander everywhere, keeping up the flame of Islam, — the hope that the day is coming, s at hand, when the white curs shall pass away, and the splendid throne which Timour won for the faithful shall again be theirs. They have their own papers, their own messengers,

anism makes converts by thousands (according to Col. Sleeman, than whom there can be no more intelligent authority) where Christianity makes but a handful; and this, he testifies, because in Mohammedanism there is no spirit of caste, while Christians have a caste of their own, and will not put converts on an equality. Do we rejoice in this great work of progress? No! one would think we were still in the time of the crusades by the way we ignore the providential value of Mohammedanism.

The one unpardonable sin is exclusiveness. Any form of religion is endangered when we bring it to the test of facts; for none on earth can bear that test. There never existed a person, nor a book, nor an institution, which did not share the merits and the drawbacks of its rivals. Granting all that can be established as to the debt of the world to the very best dispensation, the fact still remains, that there is not a single maxim, nor idea, nor application, nor triumph, that any single religion can claim as exclusively its own. Neither faith, nor love, nor truth, nor disinterestedness, nor forgiveness, nor patience, nor peace, nor equality, nor education, nor missionary effort, nor prayer, nor honesty, nor the sentiment of brotherhood, nor reverence for woman, nor the spirit of humility, nor the fact of martyrdom, nor any other good thing, is monopolized by any one or any half dozen forms of faith. All religions recognize, more or less distinctly, these principles; all do something to exemplify, something to dishonor them. Travelers find virtue in a seeming minority in all other countries, and forget that they have left it in a minority at home. A Hindoo girl, astonished at the humanity of a British officer toward her father, declared her surprise that any one could display so much kindness who did not believe in the god Vishnu. Gladwin, in his "Persian Classics," narrates

their own mail carriers, and they trust no other. Repeatedly, before the telegraph was established, their agents outstripped the fastest couriers the government could employ. The government express was carried by Mussulmans, who allowed the private messengers to get on a few hours ahead. Every dervish, moollah, or missionary, is a secret agent. This organization, which has always existed, has of late been drawn closer, partly as the result of their great mutiny, which taught the priests their hold over the soldiery, partly by the expiration of the 'century of expiation,' and partly by the marvelous revival of the Puritan element in Mohammedanism itself."

a scene which occurred in his presence between a Jew and a Mohammedan. The Mohammedan said in wrath, "If this deed of conveyance is not authentic, may God cause me to die a Jew." The Jew said, "I make my oath on the Pentateuch, and if I swear falsely I am a Mohammedan like you."

What religion stands highest in moral results if not Christianity? Yet the slave-trader belongs to Christendom as well as the saint. If we say that Christendom was not truly represented by the slaves in the hold of John Newton's slave-ship, but only by the prayers which he read every day, as he narrates, in the cabin, — then we must admit that Buddhism is not to be judged merely by the prostrations before Fo, but by the learning of its lamaseries and the beneficence of its people. The reformed Brahmoes of India complain that Christian nations force alcoholic drinks on their nation, despite their efforts; and the greater humanity of Hindoos towards animals has been, according to Dr. Hedge, a serious embarrassment to our missionaries. So men interrupt the missionaries in China, according to Coffin's late book, by asking them why, if their doctrines be true, Christian nations forced opium on an unwilling emperor, who refused to the last to receive money from the traffic? What a history has been our treatment of the American Indians? "Instead of virtues," said Cadwallader Colden, writing as early as 1727, "we have taught them vices that they were entirely free from before that time." The delegation from the Society of Friends reported last year that an Indian chief brought a young Indian before a white commissioner to give evidence, and the commissioner hesitated a little in receiving a part of the testimony, when the chief said with great emphasis, "Oh! you may believe what he says: he tells the truth: *he has never seen a white man before!*" In Southey's Wesley there is an account of an Indian whom Wesley met in Georgia, and who thus summed up his objections to Christianity: "Christian much drunk! Christian beat man! Christian tell lies! Devil Christian! Me no Christian!" * What then? All other

* See Southey's Wesley, chap. III. Report of Joint Delegation of the Society of Friends, 1869. Hedge's Primeval World of Hebrew Tradition, p. 83. Coffin's New Way Round the World, pp. 270, 308, 361. Colden's

religions show the same disparity between belief and practice, and each is safe till it tries to exclude the rest. Test each sect by its best or its worst as you will, by its high-water mark of virtue or its low-water mark of vice. But falsehood begins when you measure the ebb of any other religion against the flood-tide of your own.

There is a noble and a base side to every history. The same religion varies in different soils. Christianity is not the same in England and in Italy; in Armenia and in Ethiopia; in the Protestant and Catholic cantons of Switzerland; in Massachusetts, in Georgia, and in Utah. Neither is Buddhism the same in China, in Thibet and in Ceylon; nor Mohammedanism in Turkey and in Persia. We have no right to pluck the best fruit from one tree, the worst from another, and then say that the tree is known by its fruits. I say again, Christianity has, on the whole, produced the highest results of all, in manners, in arts, in energy. Yet when Christianity had been five centuries in the world, the world's only hope seemed to be in the superior strength and purity of pagan races. "Can we wonder," wrote Salvian (A.D. 400), "if our lands have been given over to the barbarians by God? since that which we have polluted by our profligacy the barbarians have cleansed by their chastity." * At the end of its first thousand years, Christianity could only show Europe at its lowest ebb of civilization, in a state which Guizot calls "death by the extinction of every faculty." The barbarians had only deteriorated since their conversion; the great empires were falling to pieces; and the only bright

History of the Five Indian Nations (dedication). He says also, "We have reason to be ashamed that those infidels, by our conversation and neighborhood, are become worse than they were before they knew us." It appears from this book (as from other witnesses), that one of the worst crimes now practiced by the Indians has sprung up since that day, being apparently stimulated by the brutalities practiced by whites towards Indian women. Colden says, "I have been assured that there is not an instance of their offering the least violence to the chastity of any woman that was their captive" (Vol. I., p. 9, 3d ed.). Compare Parkman's Pontiac, II., 236.

* "Cum ea quæ Romani polluerant fornicatione, nunc mundent barbari castitate."—*Salvian de Gubern. Dei.* ed. 1623, p. 254, quoted in Gilly's Vigilantius, p. 360.

spot in Europe was Mohammedan Spain, whose universities taught all Christendom science, as its knights taught chivalry. Even at the end of fifteen hundred years, the Turks, having conquered successively Jerusalem and Constantinople, seemed altogether the most powerful nation of the world; their empire was compared to the Roman empire; they were gaining all the time. You will find everywhere, in Luther's "Table-talk" for instance, how weak Christendom seemed against them in the middle of the sixteenth century; and Lord Bacon, yet later, describes them in his "Essays" as the only warlike nation in Europe, except the Spaniards. But the art of printing had been discovered, and that other new world, America; the study of Greek literature was reviving the intellect of Europe, and the tide had begun to turn. For four hundred years it has been safe for Christendom to be boastful, but, if at any time during the fifteen hundred years previous the comparison had been made, the boasting would have been the other way. It is unsafe to claim a monopoly of merit on the basis of facts that cover four centuries out of nineteen. Let us not be misled by a hasty vanity, lest some new incursion of barbarians teach us, as it taught the early Christians, to be humble.

We see what Christianity has done for Europe; but we do not remember how much Europe has done for Christianity. Take away the influence of race and climate; take away Greek literature and Mohammedan chivalry and the art of printing; set the decline of Christianity in Asia and Africa against its gain in Europe and America,—and whatever superiority may be left is not enough on which to base exclusive claims.* The

* "Neither history nor more recent experience can furnish any example of the long retention of pure Christianity by a people themselves rude and unenlightened. In all the nations of Europe, embracing every period since the second century, Christianity must be regarded as having taken the hue and complexion of the social state with which it was incorporated, presenting itself unsullied, contaminated, or corrupted, in sympathy with the enlightenment or ignorance or debasement of those by whom it had been originally embraced. The rapid and universal degeneracy of the early Asiatic churches is associated with the decline of education and the intellectual decay of the communities among whom they were established."—*Tennent's Christianity in Ceylon*, p. 273. For the influence of Mohammedanism on

recent scientific advances of the age are a brilliant theme for the rhetorician; but those who make these advances are the last men to ascribe them to the influence of any exclusive religion.

Indeed it is only very lately that the claim of superiority in civilization and the arts of life has been made in behalf of Christianity. Down to the time of the Reformation it was usual to contrast the intellectual and practical superiority of the heathen with the purely spiritual claims of the church. "The church has always been accustomed, says the Roman Catholic Digby, "to see genius and learning in the ranks opposed to her." "From the beginning of the world," said Luther, "there have always been among the heathens higher and rarer people, of greater and more exalted understanding, more excellent diligence and skill in all arts, than among Christians, or the people of God." "Do we excel in intellect, in learning, in decency of morals?" said Melancthon. "By no means. But we excel in the true knowledge and worship and adoration of God." *

Historically, of course, we are Christians, and can enjoy the advantage which that better training has given, just as the favored son of a king may enjoy his special advantages and yet admit that the less favored are equally sons. The name of Christianity only ceases to excite respect when it is used to represent any false or exclusive claims, or when it takes the place of the older and grander words, "Religion" and "Virtue." When we fully comprehend the sympathy of religions we shall deal with other faiths on equal terms. We shall cease trying to free men from one superstition by inviting them into another. The true missionaries are the men inside each religion who have outgrown its limitations. But no Christian missionary has ever yet consented to meet the men of other religions upon the com-

the revival of letters in Europe, see Andres, Origine di ogni litteratura. Jourdain, Recherches critiques sur les traductions latines d'Aristote. Schmölders, Ecoles philosophiques entre les Arabes. Forster, Mohammedanism Unveiled. Urquhart, Pillars of Hercules. Lecky's Rationalism, II., 284.

* "Quid igitur nos antecellimus? Num ingenio, doctrina, morum moderatione illos superamus? Nequaquam. Sed vera Dei agnitione, invocatione et celebratione præstamus."—*Melancthon*, quoted by Feuerbach, Essence of Christianity (Eng. tr.) p. 284. He also cites the passage from Luther.

mon ground of Theism. In Bishop Heber's time, the Hindoo reformer Swaamee Narain was teaching purity and peace, the unity of God, and the abolition of castes. Many thousands of men followed his teachings, and whole villages and districts were raised from the worst immorality by his labors, as the Bishop himself bears witness. But the good Bishop seems to have despaired of him as soon as Swaamee Narain refused conversion to Christianity, making the objection that God was not incarnated in one man, but in many. Then came Ram Mohun Roy, forty years ago, and argued from the Vedas against idolatry, caste, and the burning of widows. He also refused to be called a Christian, and the missionaries denounced him. Now comes Keshub Chunder Sen, with his generous utterances: "We profess the universal and absolute religion, whose cardinal doctrines are the Fatherhood of God and the Brotherhood of Man, and which accepts the truths of all scriptures, and honors the prophets of all nations." The movement reaches thousands whom no foreign influence could touch; yet the Methodist missionaries denounce it in the name of Christ, and even the little Unitarian mission opens against it a battery of a single gun. It is the same with our treatment of the Jews. According to Bayard Taylor, Christendom converts annually three or four Jews in Jerusalem, at a cost of $20,000 each. Nothing has been more criticised in the course of the Free Religious Association than its admission of Jews as equals on its platform; and yet the reformed Jews in America have already gone in advance of the most liberal Christian sects in their width of religious sympathy. "The happiness of man," says Rabbi Wise, in speaking for them, "depends on no creed and no book; it depends on the dominion of truth, which is the Redeemer and Savior, the Messiah and the King of Glory." *

* Rabbi Wise's remarks may be found in the Report of the Free Religious Association for 1869, p. 118. For Swaamee Narain, see Heber's Journal, II., 109–121 (Am. ed.). For Ram Mohun Roy, see his translation of the Sama Veda (Calcutta, 1816), his two tracts on the burning of widows (Calcutta, 1818, 1820), and other pamphlets. Victor Jacquemont wrote of him from Calcutta in 1830, "Il n'est pas Chrétien, quoi qu 'on en dise. . . . Les honnetes Anglais l'exècrent parce que, disent-ils, c'est un affreux déiste."—*Letters*, I., 288.

It is our happiness to live in a time when all religions are at last outgrowing their mythologies, and emancipated men are stretching out their hands to share together "the luxury of a religion that does not degrade." The progressive Brahmoes of India, the Jewish leaders in America, the Free Religious Association among ourselves, are teaching essentially the same principles, seeking the same ends. The Jewish congregations in Baltimore were the first to contribute for the education of the freedmen; the Buddhist Temple, in San Francisco, was the first edifice of that city draped in mourning after the murder of President Lincoln; the Parsees of the East sent contributions to the Sanitary Commission. The great religions of the world are but larger sects; they come together, like the lesser sects, for works of benevolence; they share the same aspirations, and every step in the progress of each brings it nearer to all the rest. For us, the door out of superstition and sin may be called Christianity; that is an historical name only, the accident of a birthplace. But other nations find other outlets; they must pass through their own doors, not through ours; and all will come at last upon the broad ground of God's providing, which bears no man's name. The reign of heaven on earth will not be called the Kingdom of Christ nor of Buddha,—it will be called the Church of God, or the Commonwealth of Man. I do not wish to belong to a religion only, but to *the* religion; it must not include less than the piety of the world.

If one insists on being exclusive, where shall he find a home? What hold has any Protestant sect among us on a thoughtful mind? They are too little, too new, too inconsistent, too feeble. What are these children of a day compared with that magnificent Church of Rome, which counts its years by centuries, and its votaries by millions, and its martyrs by myriads; with kings for confessors and nations for converts; carrying to all the earth one Lord, one faith, one baptism, and claiming for itself no less title than the Catholic, the Universal? Yet in conversing with Catholics one is again repelled by the extreme juvenility, and modernness, and scanty numbers of their church. It is the superb elder brother of our little sects, doubtless, and seems to have most of the family fortune. But the whole fortune is so small! and even the elder brother is so young! Even the Romanist ignores traditions more vast, antiquity more remote, a literature of piety more grand. His temple suffocates: give us a shrine still vaster; something than this Catholicism more catholic; not the Church of Rome, but of God and Man; a Pantheon, not a Parthenon; the true *semper, ubique, et ab omnibus*, the Religion of the Ages, Natural Religion.

I was once in a foreign cathedral when, after the three days of mourning, in Holy Week, came the final day of Hallelujah. The great church had looked dim and sad, with the innumerable windows closely curtained, since the moment when the symbolical bier of Jesus was borne to its symbolical tomb beneath the High Altar, while the three mystic candles blazed above it. There had been agony and beating of cheeks in the darkness, while ghostly processions moved through the aisles, and fearful transparencies were unrolled from the pulpit. The priests kneeled in gorgeeous robes, chanting, with their heads resting on the altar steps; the multitude hung expectant on their words. Suddenly burst forth a new chant, "Gloria in Excelsis!" In that instant every curtain was rolled aside, the cathedral was bathed in glory, the organs clashed, the bells chimed, flowers were thrown from the galleries, little birds were let loose, friends embraced and greeted one another, and we looked down upon a tumultuous sea of faces, all floating in a sunlit haze. And yet, I thought, the whole of this sublime transformation consisted in letting in the light of day! These priests and attendants, each stationed at his post, had only removed the darkness they themselves had made. Unveil these darkened windows, but remove also these darkening walls; the temple itself is but a lingering shadow of that gloom. Instead of its coarse and stifling incense, give us God's pure air, and teach us that the broadest religion is the best.

www.ingramcontent.com/pod-product-compliance
Lightning Source LLC
LaVergne TN
LVHW011145110826
845150LV00008B/2523
* 9 7 8 1 4 1 8 1 9 2 8 4 6 *